At a Glance™ Series

DVD and Lesson Book

DVD Country Guitar

Written by Mike Mueller and Chad Johnson

ISBN: 978-1-4234-4298-1

HAL•LEONARD® CORPORATION

7777 W. BLUEMOUND RD. P.O. BOX 13819 MILWAUKEE, WI 53213

Visit Hal Leonard Online at
www.halleonard.com

Table of Contents

Introduction

Welcome to *DVD Country Guitar*, from Hal Leonard's exciting At a Glance series. Not as in-depth and slow-paced as traditional method books, the material in *DVD Country Guitar* is presented in a snappy and fun manner intended to have you playing your favorite country songs and licks in virtually no time at all. Plus, the At a Glance series uses real songs by real artists to illustrate how the concepts you're learning are applied in some of the biggest hits of all time. For example, in *DVD Country Guitar*, you'll learn riffs and licks from 20 classics, including Dwight Yoakam's "Please, Please Baby," Alan Jackson's "Mercury Blues," Johnny Cash's "Folsom Prison Blues," and Chet Atkins' "Country Gentleman."

Additionally, each book in the At a Glance series comes with a DVD containing video lessons that correspond to the printed material. The DVD that accompanies this book contains four video lessons, each approximately 8 to 10 minutes in length, that correspond to each chapter in *DVD Country Guitar*. In these videos, ace instructors will show you in great detail everything from the boom-chick to chicken pickin'. As you work through the book, try to play the examples first on your own, and then check out the DVD for additional help or to see if you played it correctly. As the saying goes, "A picture is worth a thousand words," so be sure to use this invaluable tool on your quest to learning the ropes of country guitar.

COUNTRY RHYTHM GUITAR

From its early glory years with Merle Travis and Chet Atkins to its present day popularity at the hands of pickin' legends-in-waiting Brad Paisley and Keith Urban, country music has had two key elements: the best storytelling on the planet and stellar guitar playing to match.

In this first lesson, we'll examine country guitar's key rhythm techniques and approaches, from the Carter strum to the honky tonk to the boom-chick.

Cowboy Chords

Country music, from the early strums of Mother Maybelle Carter to the modern boogie of Keith Urban, is based primarily on basic open chord shapes. And when the singing cowboy Gene Autry accompanied himself using those basic, open chords in the old cowboy movies of the thirties and forties, those shapes became affectionately known as "cowboy chords," and the name has stuck ever since.

 The most common types of cowboy chords used in country music are major triads, minor triads, and dominant seventh chords. Here are the six open-position major triad chord shapes.

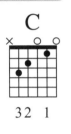 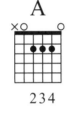 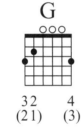  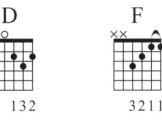

 Likewise, here are the three most commonly used open-position minor triad shapes.

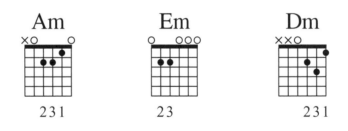

 Finally, here are the six open-position dominant seventh chord shapes.

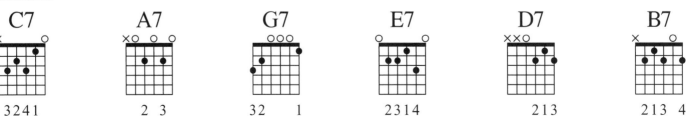

Carter Strum

In 1927, Alvin Pleasant "A.P." Carter, his wife Sara, and his sister-in-law Maybelle Carter recorded their first songs. Now, more than eighty years later, the Carter family is acknowledged as the first family of country music. And while such enduring songs as "Can the Circle Be Unbroken?," "Wildwood Flower," and "Bury Me Under the Weeping Willow" have inspired country songwriters from every generation since that time, it is Maybelle's distinctive guitar style that has been the most influential.

Until "Mother Maybelle" came along, the guitar was rarely used as a solo instrument in country music. Using a thumbpick to pluck single-note melodies on the bass strings and her fingers to strum the chords on the higher strings, Carter was the first to create the illusion of hearing two guitarists at once, thus breaking the ground for such legendary pickers as Chet Atkins and Doc Watson.

 Carter strumming breaks the chord into two elements: a bass note and a strummed chord. In its simplest form, the chord's root is typically played as a bass note on beat 1, followed by a chord strum on beat 2. Then, either the 3rd or 5th of the chord is played as a bass note on beat 3, with another chord strum on beat 4. Here's an example.

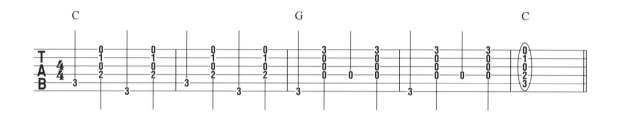

In that example, the chord strums occurred on the top four strings. Oftentimes you might only hit the top three strings, as in this example set in the key of E major.

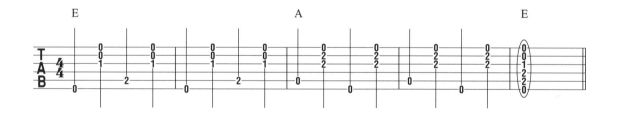

 Of course, Maybelle developed and used a number of variations on this basic approach. One of the easiest is to strum the chords in eighth notes, in down-up fashion.

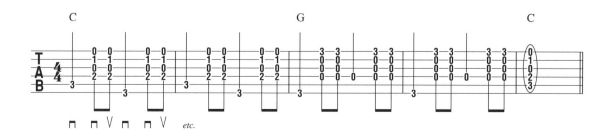

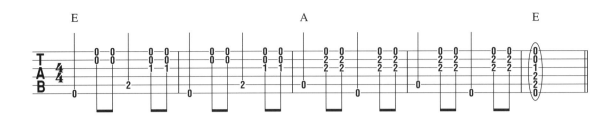

 Another accompaniment variation that Carter pioneered was adding ornaments such as hammer-ons and pull-offs to the bass line. This kind of move, which adds energy and momentum to the progression, was widely adopted by bluegrass guitarists to make their already uptempo parts really sizzle.

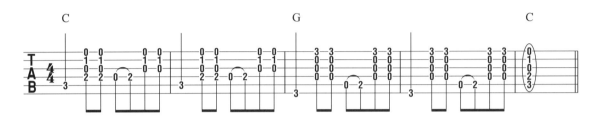

Bass Lines

 So far, the bass portions of the Carter strum variations have consistently alternated with the chord strums, but Maybelle also used *walking* bass lines, especially between chord changes, to shake things up. This next example navigates C and F chord changes with ascending and descending bass lines leading into each change.

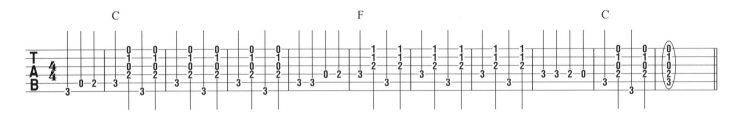

COUNTRY CHORD PROGRESSIONS

Country music, like blues and early rock 'n' roll, is often written within the construct of simple three- and four-chord progressions. For example, a song like Johnny Cash's classic "Folsom Prison Blues" contains only E, A, and B7 chords. These are the I, IV, and V chords, respectively, in the key of E major. This I–IV–V combination is the most popular chord family in country music.

To determine the I, IV, and V chords in any key, first spell out that key's major scale. For example, in C major, the scale is:

Key of C: C–D–E–F–G–A–B

Then find the first, fourth, and fifth notes—here, C, F, and G, respectively—and play their respective major chords: C, F, and G. Note that the fifth, or V chord, may be played as either a major chord or a dominant 7th chord (i.e., G, or G7).

Now, for an actual example of the Carter strum, I can think of no better place to look than at a Carter Family classic: "Wildwood Flower."

"WILDWOOD FLOWER"
Carter Family

Words and Music by
A.P. Carter

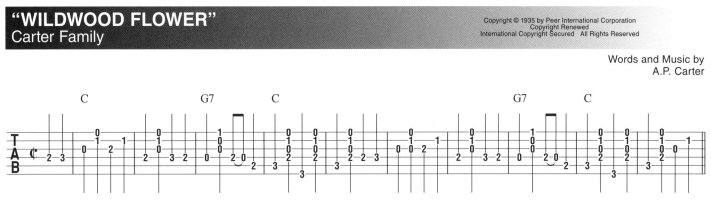

Travis Picking

Named for country guitar legend Merle Travis, *Travis picking* is a technique integral to country rhythm guitar. It's a fingerstyle technique that, when mastered, can make the guitar sound like an orchestra.

Interestingly, Merle Travis's fingerstyle approach included just his thumb and index finger. When Chet Atkins heard Travis performing on a radio show one night, he was blown away and decided he just had to learn how to play like that. Atkins, however, mistakenly thought that Travis was using his thumb and *two* fingers—index and middle. So Atkins pursued his fingerstyle mastery in that manner, later incorporating as many as three and four fingers into the technique as well.

The key to effective Travis picking is a rock-solid thumb, keeping the quarter note-driven bass line firmly in the pocket. Many teachers suggest isolating the bass line and getting it "under your thumb" before incorporating your fingers on the melody and chords. Using this approach, you might first want to work on exercises like these, to get your thumb moving. This first one contains a bass line alternating between two strings on each chord.

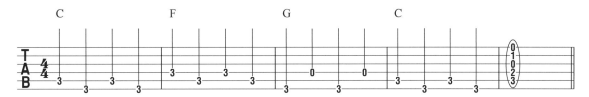

Alternatively, some Travis picking bass lines involve notes on three strings.

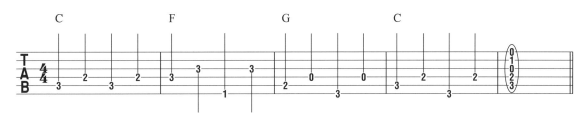

Still other players, like fingerstyle master Adrian Legg, suggest learning both thumb and fingers at the same time, which is how it's presented here. You can use whichever approach you want—either way, it's a must-know technique.

Here's our first full-on example. Use your thumb to play all the notes on the bottom three strings, your index finger for the notes on the third string, and your middle finger for the notes on the second string.

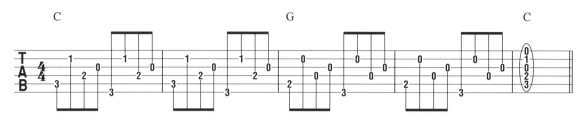

The next step in mastering Travis picking is plucking bass and melody notes at the same time. This variation provides a more solid harmonic foundation. Here's an example, this time using a dominant seventh chord, for a little of that old-timey vibe.

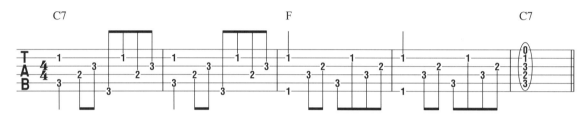

OK, now let's vary the rhythm and placement of dyad attacks, so that your fingers don't get comfortable in just one groove. In this C7–G7 progression, you'll encounter consecutive dyads on beats 1 and 2. Use your thumb for all notes on strings 6–4, your index on string 3, middle on string 2, and ring on string 1.

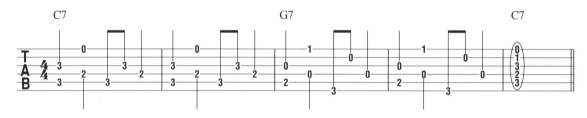

Now, here's an example of Travis picking in the style of Chet Atkins. Notice how the fretboard is divided into three distinct parts: melody notes on top, bass notes on the bottom, and 3rds dyads in the middle.

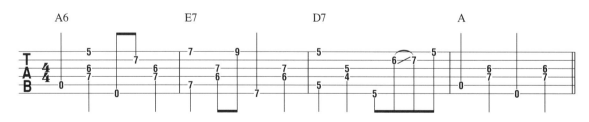

Our next Travis picking example comes from the man himself. "Sixteen Tons," written by Merle Travis in 1947, is a little unusual, as it is set in the key of A minor. Wrap your fret hand's thumb around the neck to fret the low F note on beat 1 of measure 2.

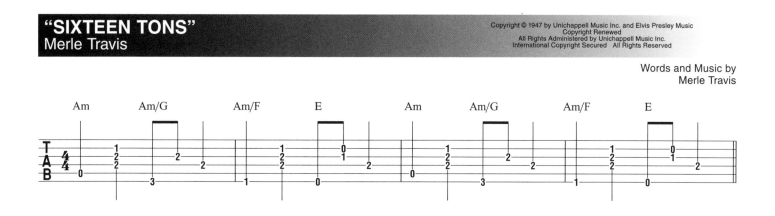

Words and Music by
Merle Travis

Boom-Chucka

When Johnny Cash recorded such hits as "Folsom Prison Blues" and "Ring of Fire," his guitarist, Luther Perkins, unwittingly immortalized the boom-chucka rhythm. Based on the Carter strum, which comprises bass notes alternating with chord strums, the boom-chucka rhythm uses all single notes, in a quarter-and-two-eighths rhythmic pattern that recalls a "boom-chucka" sound. To best cop the traditional boom-chucka vibe, use a slight palm mute and add a touch of slapback echo or delay.

Here's the basic idea, set in a typical country I–V progression in the key of E.

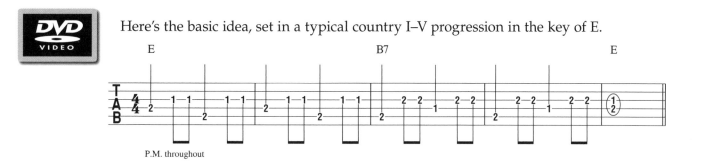

Now, we can take it a step further and, as in Carter strumming, introduce a walking bass line between chord changes. To really get the feel of this all-important rhythm technique, here's a 20-bar country chorus in C.

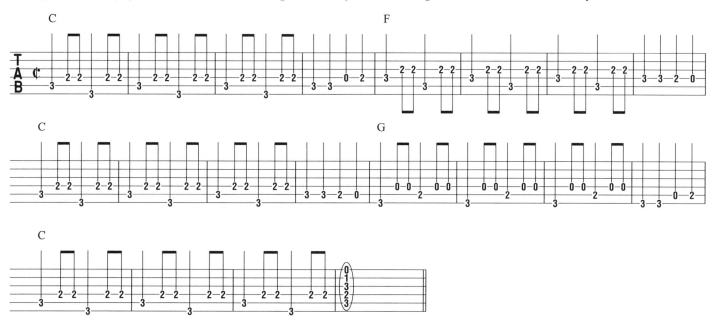

OK, by now you should be ready to back the man in black himself, so step into the great Luther Perkins' shoes and take your boom-chucka for a spin on "Folsom Prison Blues." This excerpt is taken from measure 13 of the verse, which is where Perkins kicks in his famous dead-string boom-chucka lick.

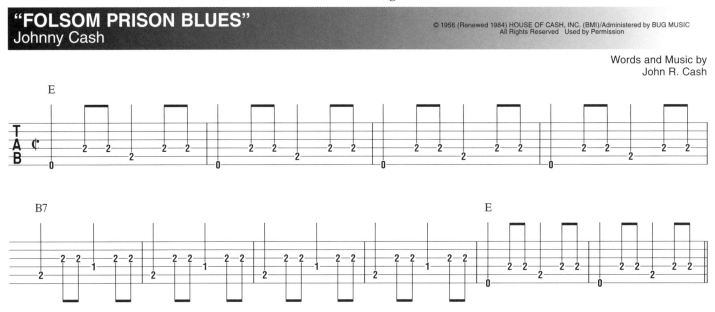

A popular variation on the single-note boom-chucka is applying the same concept to the Carter strum, in which you play a single bass note followed by a staccato chord strum, thus creating a *boom-chick* sound. Typically, the bass note alternates between the root and 5th, and a slight palm mute is applied throughout.

One of the best examples of the boom-chick sound is the Hank Williams classic, "Hey, Good Lookin'."

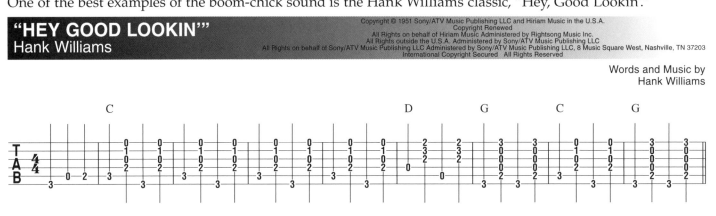

Boogie Woogie Rhythms

Country and rock music actually have quite a bit in common, which makes sense seeing as rock 'n' roll was born out of a mix of early country and blues. One of its most fertile common grounds is the boogie-woogie rhythm. Originating in nineteenth-century logging camps in the South, it was later cemented as a musical style by blues pianists like George Thomas and Pinetop Smith. The first country boogie woogie song was "Boogie Woogie" by Johnny Barfield in 1939. By 1945, the floodgates had opened, and hits like the Delmore Brothers' "Freight Train Boogie" and Arthur Smith's "Guitar Boogie" showed that country boogie was here to stay, paving the way for rock guitar pioneer Chuck Berry to make the sound immortal.

Here is a countrified take on the classic Chuck Berry boogie riff. Note the half-step approach to both the I and the IV chords. This is a very common country move.

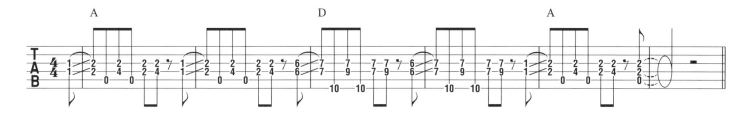

Another way that country guitarists employ the boogie rhythm is through a walking (more like *sprinting*) single-note bass line to create a boogie *riff*. To give these lines their familiar country twang, country guitarists typically use the ♭3rd as a passing tone to the major 3rd, similar to the famous Lester Flatt runs in bluegrass guitar.

This next example in the key of A major showcases the ♭3rd–3rd (C–C♯) move quite prominently. For best results, dig in with the pick.

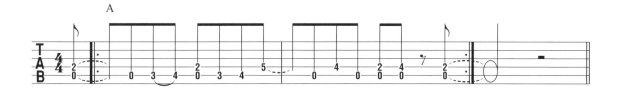

For an example of just how moving a boogie riff can be, we turn to one of the great barnstorming riffs of all time—Commander Cody's smokin' "Hot Rod Lincoln." In this riff, we see the I, IV, and V chords (E, A, and B) in rapid succession. The E and A are in open position, but the B chord offers up a challenging shift up to fourth position.

"HOT ROD LINCOLN"
Commander Cody

Words and Music by W.S. Stevenson
and Charley Ryan

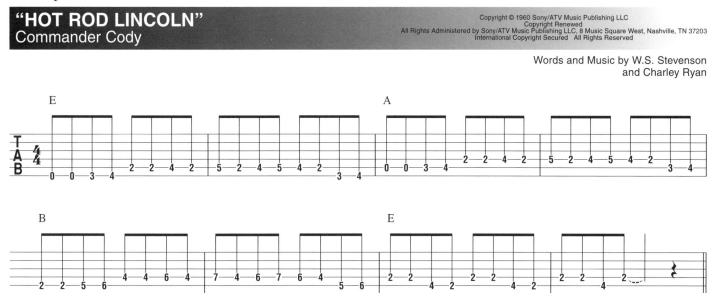

Hybrid Picking

So far, we used a flatpick to play some Carter strums and boogie riffs, and we used our fingers for some tasty Travis picking. But there's one more approach that country pickers keep in their twangy arsenals, and that's using both at the same time! The *hybrid picking* technique typically involves picking single notes with your pick, or plectrum, and plucking either single notes or chord partials with a combination of your pick hand's middle, ring, and pinky fingers.

 Here's a modern country-style riff using hybrid picking. Play it slightly behind the beat for added Southern charm, and be sure to really dig in with your fingers on the chord stabs.

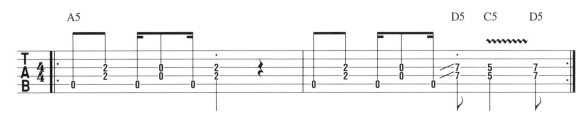

And here's another hot little hybrid riff in D that makes use of pull-offs and a few pseudo banjo rolls—two techniques often intertwined with the hybrid style. The right-hand fingering is given for this one, as it can be a bit tricky.

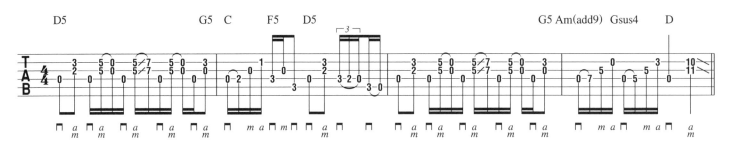

Now let's check out the hybrid style in the real world. On Alan Jackson's "Mercury Blues," Brent Mason pulls off this tasty rhythm fill using an open unison string (the open G) and a first inversion G7 roll before snapping off a tonic D5 chord.

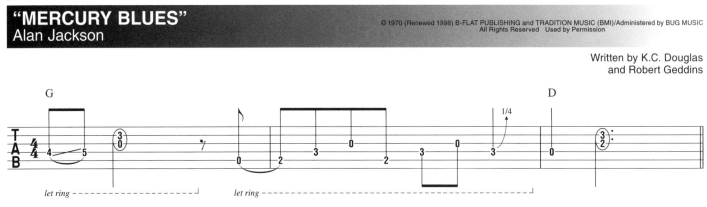

"MERCURY BLUES"
Alan Jackson

Written by K.C. Douglas
and Robert Geddins

Be sure to check out recordings from country's legendary artists like Merle Travis, Chet Atkins, Jerry Reed, and Johnny Cash as well as modern artists like Toby Keith, Dwight Yoakam, Keith Urban, and Brad Paisley for a nice cross-section of country rhythm guitar styles.

COUNTRY LEAD GUITAR

For the past 50 years, some of the world's hottest lead guitarists have been country pickers. Virtuosos like Jimmy Bryant, Chet Atkins, Joe Maphis, Danny Gatton, Albert Lee, Brent Mason, and Brad Paisley have all advanced the art of lead guitar, often by playing things no one had ever thought possible.

Country lead guitar has a very recognizable sound, and much of that is due to the scales, phrasing, techniques, and tones country guitarists tend to use. Without these traits, many country licks could be mistaken for blues or rock licks, while others could easily pass for jazz licks. Some, however, are pure countrified. For those licks, the information in this chapter should be considered prerequisite.

Major Pentatonic Scale

The first must-know scale in country music is the *major pentatonic scale*. Comprising the first, second, third, fifth, and sixth degrees of the major scale, these five notes are at the heart of countless country solos.

 Here's the most common fingering of the major pentatonic scale in the key of A.

If that pattern seems familiar, it's because it's also the most popular fingering for the F# minor pentatonic scale, which is the relative minor of A major. This simply means that the two scales share the same notes, but they have different root notes. In other words, A major pentatonic treats the note A as the root, or tonic, and F# minor pentatonic treats the note F# as the root.

 Here's another popular major pentatonic scale pattern. This one involves position shifts via several slides.

 Now, let's take a look at a few major pentatonic licks using these scale patterns. This first lick descends the major pentatonic box pattern. Keep that bend in measure 1 very precise and accurate; this is one of the key factors that separates this from a rock lick.

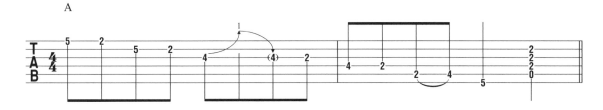

 Here's a lick that uses the top three strings of the extended major pentatonic pattern. Note the pre-bend that kicks off the lick; this is a very popular country move. Again, be sure the intonation is accurate on the bend.

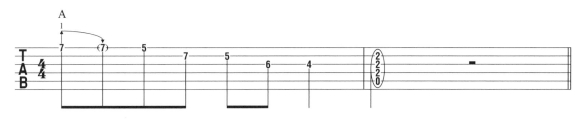

Another commonly mined scale form for the A major pentatonic scale is found in ninth position. Here's what it looks like:

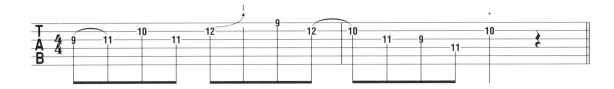

You'll hear country pickers lasso licks from this form all the time—things like this.

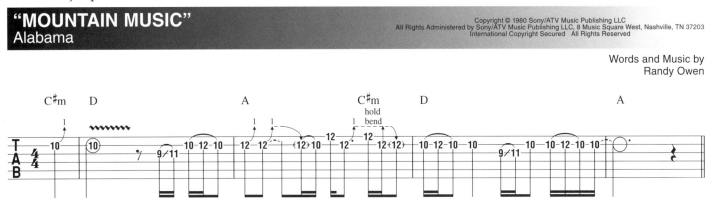

In Alabama's classic pop country anthem "Mountain Music," guitarist Jeff Cook camps out in this ninth-position A major pentatonic form for a memorable, melodic excursion.

"MOUNTAIN MUSIC"
Alabama

Words and Music by
Randy Owen

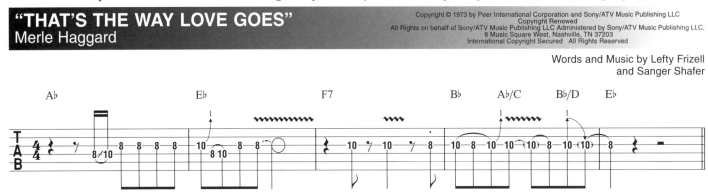

Remember, these scale shapes are moveable so, although we've been playing these licks in A, you can play them in any key just by moving them around.

Check out how Reggie Young milks the E♭ major pentatonic scale during his solo on Merle Haggard's 1983 hit, "That's the Way Love Goes." There's nothing fancy here—just extremely tasty note choice and a gorgeous touch.

"THAT'S THE WAY LOVE GOES"
Merle Haggard

Words and Music by Lefty Frizell
and Sanger Shafer

Country Composite Scale

While the major pentatonic scale is a good starting point for creating country licks and solos, if you *really* want to sound country, you need to know the *country composite scale*. This is just a fancy name for a major pentatonic scale with an added ♭3rd. Here's what that scale pattern looks like in the key of A.

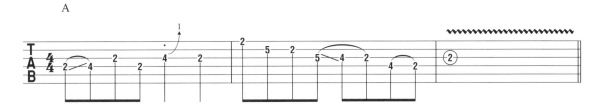

If you're a blues or rock player, you'll no doubt recognize this as the F♯ blues scale. That's another way of looking at it; the country composite scale is the same as the blues scale built from the relative minor. Again, it's just that, for the A country composite scale, we're treating A as the root note, so most of our phrases will tend to resolve there instead of F♯.

Here's a snappy lick from this form that sounds best with hybrid picking. For those staccato notes, use your fingers to pull up on the string, allowing it to slap against the fretboard to create the desired pop.

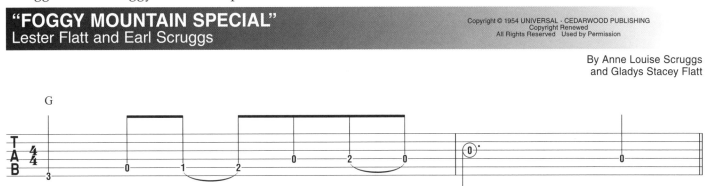

One of the most popular licks to employ the country composite scale is known as the "Lester Flatt run." Flatt was a bluegrass guitarist, but his signature lick successfully crossed over to country as well. The Flatt run is most commonly played in open position in the key of G. Here's how it originally appeared in the Flatt and Scruggs classic, "Foggy Mountain Special."

"FOGGY MOUNTAIN SPECIAL"
Lester Flatt and Earl Scruggs

By Anne Louise Scruggs
and Gladys Stacey Flatt

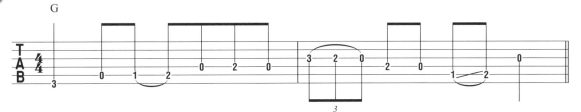

Over the years, folks have added to and dressed up this lick. A common variation you hear may sound something like this:

In the ninth position, the A country composite scale looks like this:

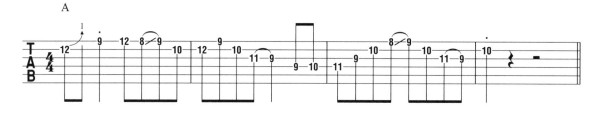

And here's what you may hear in that area. Notice how slides are employed for the chromatic notes, as heard in the Lester Flatt run. This is a very common move in country and jazz as well.

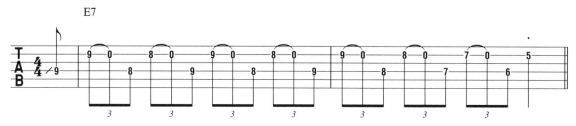

Sixths

The 6th interval is another very common tool in the country player's shed. Only country guitarists like to add a little twist—open strings. This will work best in the country-approved "open-string" keys of A, G, E, D, and C, but feel free to try it out in other keys for some interesting sounds.

This first lick in the key of E involves slightly muted pull-offs to the open B string for a chicken pickin'-style sound (see Lesson 4 for more on chicken pickin').

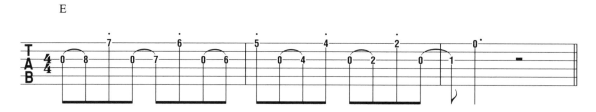

This next lick, also in the key of E, uses hammer-ons from the open G string. Make sure to snap that high E string hard!

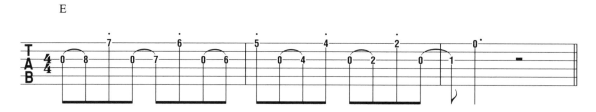

One of the kings of this type of thing is Pete Anderson, guitarist and producer with Dwight Yoakam. Check out the soaring chromatic lick in "Please, Please Baby," where he works his way from open position all the way up to sixteenth. Nabbing every fret along the way combined with open strings, the lick sounds like a wobbly, puttering rocket set against a cartoon sky. Though it's hard to tell out of context, the lick is in the key of E and begins on the V chord, B. Hybrid picking is an absolute must here.

"PLEASE, PLEASE BABY"
Dwight Yoakam

Words and Music by
Dwight Yoakam

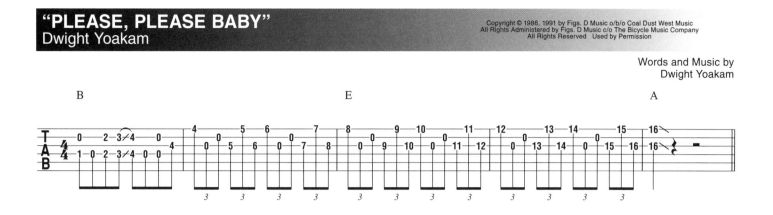

Telestrangler Jerry Donahue peels off a cascading, descending 6ths lick in his show-stopping rendition of Jerry Reed's "The Claw." Again, use hybrid picking and be sure to allow all the strings to ring as long as possible to get the maximum effect.

"THE CLAW"
Jerry Donahue

By Jerry Reed

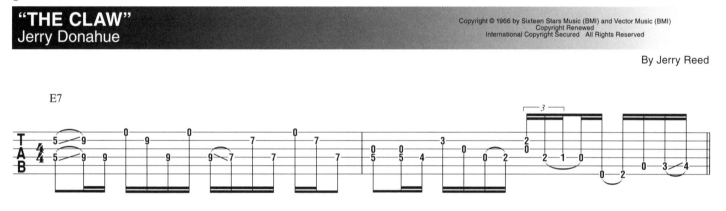

Open-String Licks

As those 6ths licks illustrate, country guitarists just love to use open strings in their licks. In that spirit, our next lick utilizes hammer-ons from open strings and banjo roll-style hybrid picking to go from the open low E string up two octaves to the twelfth-fret E on the first string. It's a great lick for covering a lot of sonic ground quickly.

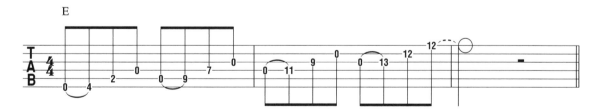

Notice that, even though the open G string isn't in the key of E major, it still sounds great in a lick like this.

Here's another nifty little run in E that makes a great closing lick. Keep those fret-hand fingers arched, so the strings can ring throughout.

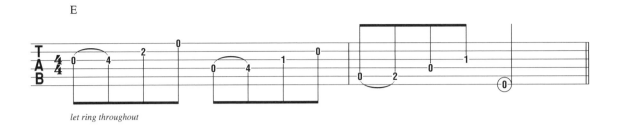

let ring throughout

When you talk about open-string licks, it's only a matter of time before Chet's name comes up. "Mr. Guitar" recorded *Neck and Neck* with Mark Knopfler in the early nineties, a guitarist's dream album overflowing with brilliant fretwork from both. During one of his many breaks on "There'll Be Some Changes Made," Chet plucks this ultra-hip, banjo-roll, open-string blossom to round out the form.

"THERE'LL BE SOME CHANGES MADE"
Chet Atkins & Mark Knopfler

Words by Billy Higgins
Music by W. Benton Overstreet

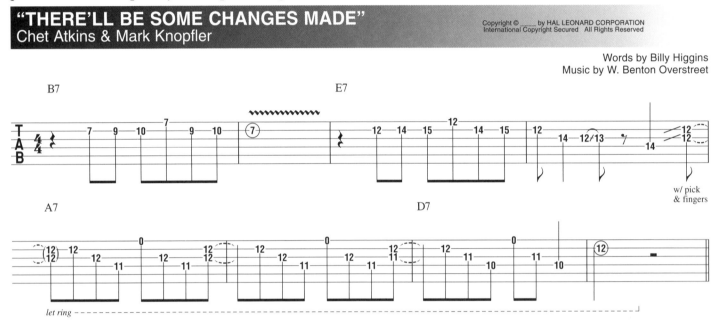

let ring

THUMBPICKS

Some players, such as Chet Atkins and Nashville session king Brent Mason, prefer to use thumbpicks. Doing so frees up all four fingers of the pick hand and still allows flatpicking when desired. (The thumbpick can be used as a regular flatpick as well.) If you're already adept at straight fingerstyle playing, the thumbpick provides a nice transition to flatpicking. They take a bit of getting used to if you've never tried one, but two of the greatest country pickers of all time can't be wrong. Give 'em a try!

Pedal Steel Licks

Another key aspect to country lead guitar is emulating the pedal steel guitar. Pedal steel players bend strings by using mechanical foot pedals, resulting in very precise intonation. This is definitely something to keep in mind in order to help achieve a country sound. Work on getting your bends in tune quickly and precisely; doing that alone will often make the difference between a rock/blues lick and a country lick. We'll study these licks more in depth in Lesson 4, but we'll touch upon a few key aspects here.

The first, and easiest, way to emulate a pedal steel is with *oblique bends*, where one string is bent against another one that's held steady. Here's a countrified example using hybrid picking for that snappy, country sound.

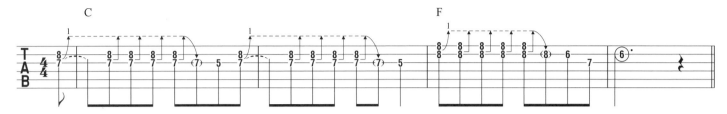

 Our next lick features oblique bends on non-adjacent strings, with the bend held over several beats. The key to this kind of lick is maintaining pitch on the bent note while fretting notes on other strings. You may want to experiment with different fingerings to see which works best.

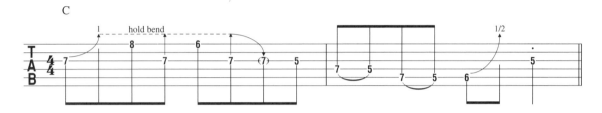

Behind-the-Nut Bends

 If you find standard oblique bends too easy, it's time to step up to the big daddy of bending: behind the nut. You'll need a Tele- or Strat-style guitar without a locking nut to pull this off—not to mention a decent threshold for pain in the beginning! Set in the key of A, this lick covers the V–IV–I changes at the end of a 12-bar form. Check it out.

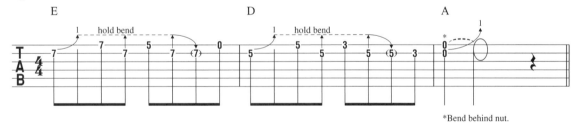

Hands down, the king of behind-the-nut bends is Jerry Donahue. Check out this finger-twister from "The Claw" used to handle the V–IV–I changes in A.

"THE CLAW"
Jerry Donahue

By Jerry Reed

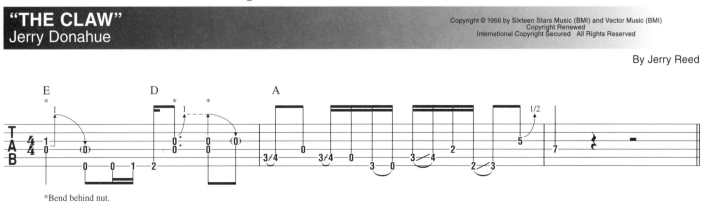

Banjo Rolls

The final country lead guitar technique in this lesson is the *banjo roll*. Our first banjo roll comes from perhaps the greatest banjoist of all time: Earl Scruggs. Use hybrid picking and be sure to let all the notes ring out.

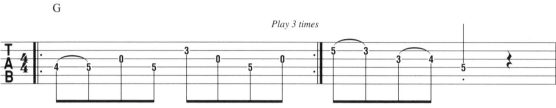

This next banjo roll has become synonymous with country guitar. This too is a three-string roll, but this time it's on the top three strings, with three triple stops leading the way. Again, use hybrid picking and let the notes ring throughout.

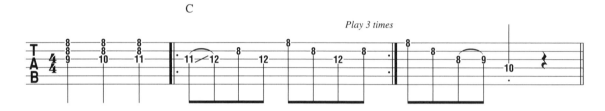

Chet Atkins, one of the true masters of the banjo roll (let alone dozens of other techniques), whipped out a doozy to close "Country Gentleman."

"COUNTRY GENTLEMAN"
Chet Atkins

By Chet Atkins
and Boudleaux Bryant

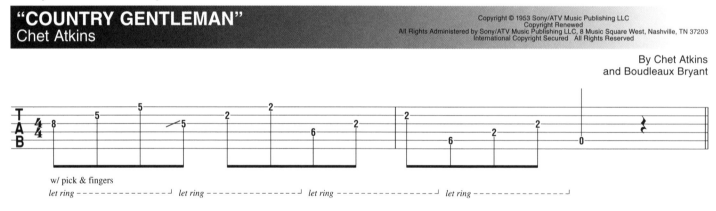

Well, that's all the cornbread we've got time for in this lesson. Be sure to listen to such masters as Chet Atkins, Joe Maphis, Danny Gatton, Albert Lee, Brent Mason, and Brad Paisley for a pretty good picture of what hot country guitar is all about.

CHICKEN PICKIN'

Recently, hot country lead guitar has experienced a rebirth among guitar players across several genres. Even rough 'n' gruff metal guitar god Zakk Wylde has reportedly been copping Albert Lee licks in his spare time. So with country lead guitar finding new warmth under the spotlight, there's a whole new slew of players out there asking, "Just what the heck is this chicken pickin' thing anyway?" Well, you've come to the right place. In this lesson, we'll look at several ways to coax that tricky barnyard cluck from *your* guitar's strings.

Chicken pickin' is as much about the sound as it is about the technique. So before we delve into the technique itself, you need to get your twang on. The bridge pickup on a Fender Telecaster is the vehicle of choice for most cluckers, but you can get by using most any solidbody guitar on the bridge pickup setting, preferably with a single-coil. You'll also want to use light-gauge strings—no heavier than .010s.

Next, set your amp for a clean tone with extra treble, and if you have reverb on the amp, crank it up about twice as high as your normal setting. Finally, if you've got a delay pedal, set it for a nice slapback echo effect. Now you're ready to start cluckin'.

Basic Technique

 Chicken pickin' emulates the "cluck" and subsequent "squawk" sounds a chicken makes, hence the name. To create this sound on a guitar, you play a short, muted note followed by a loud, sharply plucked ringing one. Here's how to do it.

Start with a single note; fret the C at the fifth fret on the third string. Now, rest your pick hand's middle finger against the third string so that it's muted. Then, play the muted note using your pick. That's the "cluck."

Next, sound the C note by pulling the string upward with your middle finger and allowing it to snap back against the fretboard. That's the "squawk."

Now, slowly repeat the process, and gradually build up the tempo. *Voila!* You're chicken pickin'!

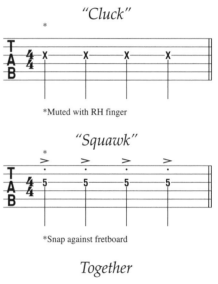

"Cluck"

Muted with RH finger

"Squawk"

Snap against fretboard

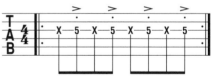

Together

 Now that we've got the basic idea, let's get down to some Colonel-approved chicken pickin' licks that are fingerlickin' good. Building on the basic chicken pickin' technique, here's a Chet Atkins-style lick in C that features a chromatically descending line on top.

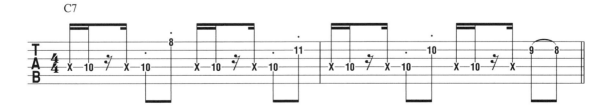

You can also incorporate this basic, alternating muted-squawking sound into double-stop licks, where you mute only the lower string of the pair.

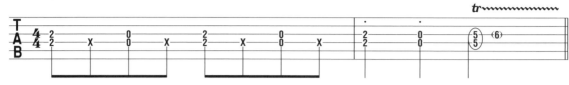

ALTERNATIVE CLUCKING

Another way of getting the "cluck" sound is to simply pick a string that's muted by the *fret hand*, which is accomplished by lightly touching the string, but not pushing down far enough to create a distinguishable note. This is especially useful in faster passages where it may be difficult to get a pick-hand finger in place to mute the string in time. The alternative method doesn't sound quite as good as the standard one, but it creates the essence of the sound and will certainly do in a pinch.

Oddly enough, one of the best-known straightforward chicken pickin' licks of all time isn't a country lick at all—or at least it wasn't played on a country record. Playing with the James Gang in 1969, rock guitar legend Joe Walsh laid down some chicken pickin' in "Funk 49" that was downright golden. This lick, inspired by Walsh, uses a similar gradual release from a whole-step bend. You can use this type of lick in virtually any hot country solo setting.

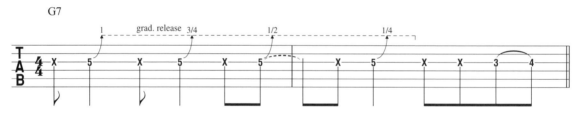

In Alan Jackson's "Mercury Blues," Brent Mason wraps up his solo over the D blues form with this gem. Keep the muted notes nice and tight, and really snap those oblique bends.

"MERCURY BLUES"
Alan Jackson

Written by K.C. Douglas
and Robert Geddins

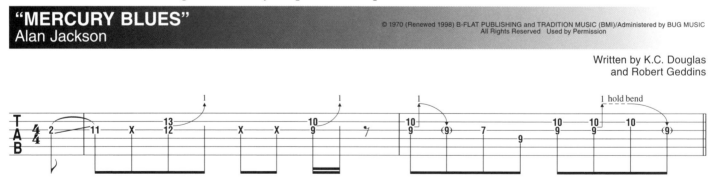

So far, we've been muting the same string as the sounded notes to produce the chicken pickin' sound. Our next lick, in A Mixolydian, uses a different approach, placing the mutes on a ghost string. To execute this lick effectively, use palm muting on the muted strings.

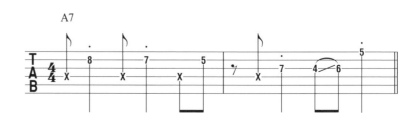

Country music is a decidedly American music form, yet two of its greatest guitarists were born in the U.K. One is Albert Lee, who will be attended to later. The other is Ray Flacke, a monster picker who's played with everyone from Ricky Skaggs and Marty Stuart to Emmylou Harris and Travis Tritt. This next lick, in the style of Flack, demonstrates his unique approach to double stops flanked by muted clucks.

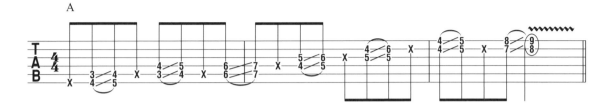

Check out how Flacke dresses up the Ricky Scaggs hit "Heartbroke" during the solo with an ascending chicken pickin' line that climbs along with the Em–F#m–G progression before breaking off into more bluesy clucking with oblique bends.

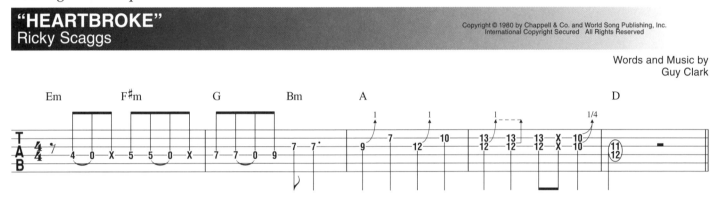

"HEARTBROKE"
Ricky Scaggs

Words and Music by
Guy Clark

A LITTLE GOES A LONG WAY

Don't feel that you need to overdo it with the chicken pickin' technique; one well-placed cluck can flavor an entire phrase. Some players end up trying to cram muted clucks in between every note and, while some of the examples in this chapter do contain a fair share of clucks in order to help develop the technique, they're not often used to that extreme in the real world.

For example, below are two versions of the same lick. Notice that B still essentially sounds like A, even though it's missing the second clucked note.

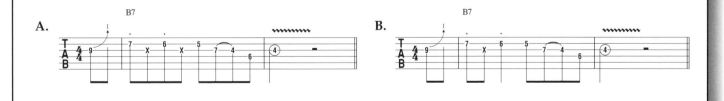

This isn't to say that you shouldn't fill up your phrases with clucks if you want to. It's just that you don't necessarily *have to* in order to get the chicken pickin' sound.

Open-String Approach

There are ways to produce the chicken pickin' sound without overt string muting. One way is to use rapid-fire hammer-ons from and pull-offs to open strings. Combine that move with a large interval like a sixth, and you're really cookin'!

 This next lick utilizes hammer-ons from the open D string to craft a G Mixolydian-blues hybrid lick. You can use either your middle or ring finger to snap the notes on the B string—whichever is more comfortable for you. Be sure to get a slight palm mute on the D string, for best chicken pickin' effect.

G7

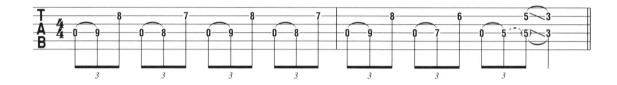

 Inspired by country metal shredder John 5, this lick also uses 6ths intervals; only here you pull off to the open B string. Again, apply a slight palm mute to the D string.

E7

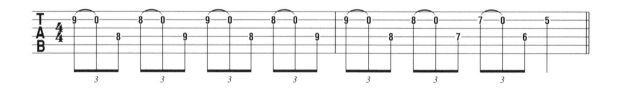

 As an alternative to 6ths intervals, you can use adjacent-string double stops, like the 3rds in this lick, to similar clucky effect.

D7

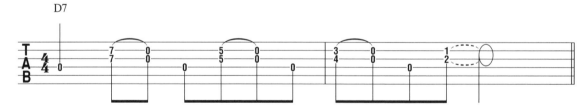

 Probably the most highly respected hot country guitar player in all of guitardom is U.K. import Albert Lee. He can go from soulful, crying B-bender balladry to smokin' roadhouse chicken pickin' at the drop of a dime and do it all with phrasing to die for. This first Albert Lee-style lick is an A Mixolydian-blues hybrid double-stop chicken pickin' casserole.

A7

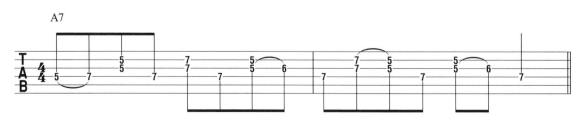

Here's an Albert Lee/Jerry Donahue classic that has been ably adopted by the great Steve Morse as well. You can almost see a chicken bobbing its head back and forth as it grazes the farmyard.

With lightning-fast 16th-note triplets picked on the G string followed immediately by a snappy 6th on the high E string, this lick can tie your fingers into pretzel knots at first. Start slowly enough to get your fret hand and picking hand in sync, and then gradually work up the tempo.

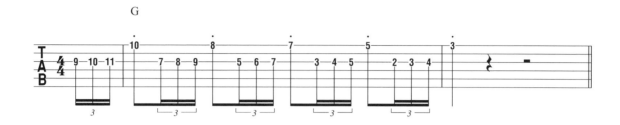

Here's Albert clucking his way through a C7–F7 progression in "Bullish Boogie," combining open strings with double stops and snaky chromatic lines. Be sure to pop those double stops with your fingers.

"BULLISH BOOGIE"
Albert Lee

Written by Albert Lee

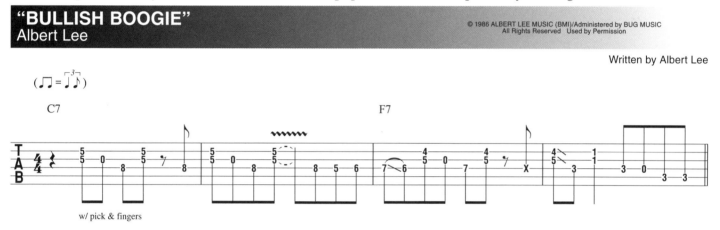

w/ pick & fingers

PEDAL STEEL LICKS

In recent years, country guitar techniques have grabbed the ears of guitarists everywhere looking to add fresh licks to their arsenals. And there are few sounds as heart-wrenching and attention-grabbing as that of well-executed pedal steel licks. In this lesson, we're going to explore the secrets to making your guitar cry and sing, pedal-steel style.

In case you're not familiar with the instrument, a pedal steel guitar is played with a solid metal bar slid across the strings, similar to the way we play slide guitar. There are pedals attached to the strings that, when depressed, raise the pitch of its particular string by a predetermined amount—usually a half or whole step. The pedals are very precise, which is one reason it's difficult to emulate the pedal steel. We have to be very precise with our bends.

Practice the following lick and check your intonation against a fretted note to be sure you're accurately matching the pitch. Try to imagine that the strings are being guided to the correct pitch mechanically.

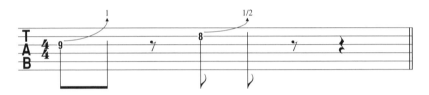

Since we don't have the luxury of the foot pedal, our fretting hands have to sometimes simultaneously fret some notes while bending others! But that's enough whining; it's time to suck it up and make your *guitar* whine—pedal steel style!

Oblique Bends

There are two primary factors to successful pedal steel licks: pitch accuracy and oblique motion. Using simple oblique bends, we can start working on both of those elements. Simply defined, an oblique bend is one in which two or more notes are played, one being a bent note. Here are a few of the most common oblique bends in country music.

This first one, from the major pentatonic scale, takes place on string set 2–3.

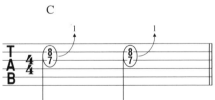

And here's a pedal steel lick that uses this bend. Make sure you hit your target note on the bend, and then hold it steady for this lick. Also, be sure to use hybrid picking. Pedal steelers play with fingerpicks and attack all the strings at once instead of stumming. This is a big part of that snappy country sound.

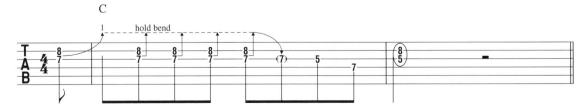

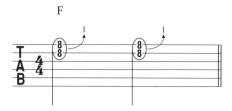

Now let's move the same oblique bend over to string set 1–2. The shape changes of course, due to the tuning of the guitar.

And here's the same lick as before, transposed up a 4th to F. As before, use hybrid picking for this lick.

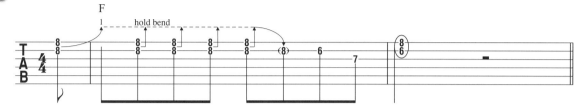

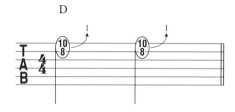

With those two bends under your fingers, you've got the necessary tools to cop tons of pro licks, but who wants to stop there? With one more bend on string set 1–2, you can really start getting into pedal steel territory. Here's what it looks like. This one is probably best fingered with your pinky on string 1 and your second finger, supported by the first behind, handling the bend on string 2.

Let's take a look at how that one can be incorporated.

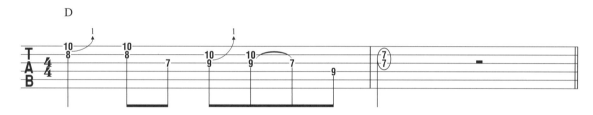

Of course, you don't have the strike the strings of the oblique bend at the same time, as guitarist Jeff Cook demonstrates with this tasteful excerpt from Alabama's "Mountain Music." Notice how he uses the same bend in two different positions to play the changes.

"MOUNTAIN MUSIC"
Alabama

Words and Music by
Randy Owen

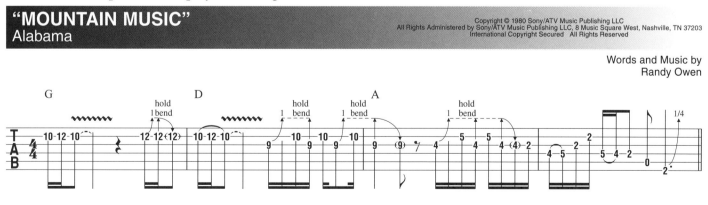

In Travis Tritt's rowdy waltz, "Here's a Quarter (Call Someone Who Cares)," Richard Bennett shows how it's really done, making use of all three bends we've looked at thus far.

"HERE'S A QUARTER (CALL SOMEONE WHO CARES)"
Travis Tritt

Words and Music by
Travis Tritt

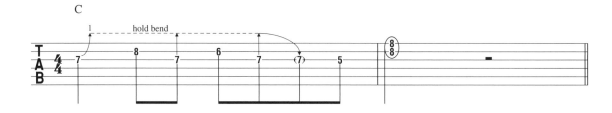

The next oblique bend lick involves playing more than one note on the stationary strings while holding the bend. The challenge with this type of pedal steel lick is maintaining pitch on the whole-step bend while changing fretted notes on the stationary string.

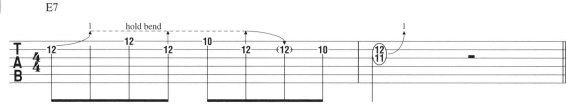

Here's a similar lick, this time on string set 1–2 and over an E7 chord.

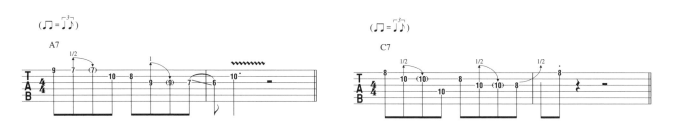

THE POWER OF PRE-BENDS

Sometimes pedal steelers already have a pedal depressed when they strike a string, then they release the pedal, thus lowering the pitch. Pre-bends on the guitar can do great job simulating this effect, even with single-note lines. It takes some preparation and a good deal of thinking ahead, but it's a skill well worth developing. Here are a couple of examples using this technique.

Remember, absolute precision on the pre-bends is essential in achieving a convincing pedal steel sound!

Oblique bends do not always need to be performed on adjacent strings. You can create some very interesting sounds by skipping a string or two. Here's a nice A7 lick demonstrating this concept that requires you to hold a third-string bend while fretting notes on both the first and second strings.

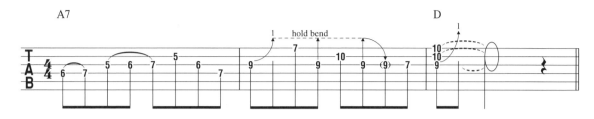

This lick in the key of B makes a great intro lick. Remember to focus on maintaining the pitch of that bend and experiment with different fret-hand fingerings if necessary. For added country flavor, allow the final three notes of the lick to ring out to form a first-inversion B chord.

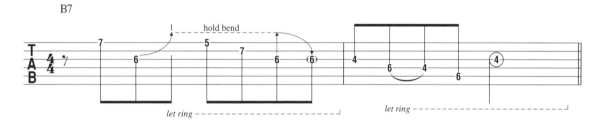

The funny thing about country is that, even though the instrumentation is largely handled by session players, there are still plenty of vocalists that can tear up a Tele as well. Among them are Brad Paisley, Marty Stuart, Keith Urban, and Vince Gill, to name only a few. In "One More Last Chance," Vince lets loose with a classic oblique pedal steel move similar to our previous lick.

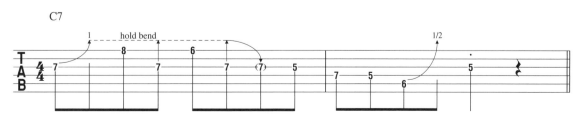

Words and Music by Gary Nicholson
and Vince Gill

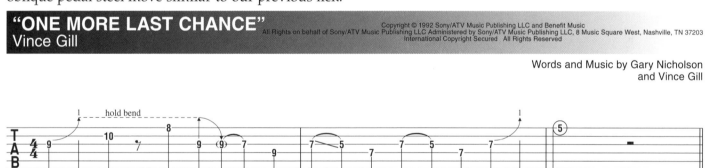

This next lick moves into new fretboard territory, in that it requires you to bend and hold the fifth string at the end of the phrase. It's only a half-step bend, so it shouldn't be too taxing, but take your time getting the pitch right. You'll need to pull the fifth string downward, toward the floor, to achieve the bend. This is typically the best way to bend the lower strings.

Multiple String Bends

So far, we've focused on bending just one string to create pedal steel licks, but you can bend more than one string with some tantalizing results. This parallel 6ths lick requires a simultaneous half-step bend on the first string and whole-step bend on the third. Here's a tip: if you keep the strings parallel, you should get the correct pitches. Use your second and third fingers, respectively, to execute the bends, and give it a country shuffle feel. The lick itself makes a great intro to a slow Carter-strummed A7 chord.

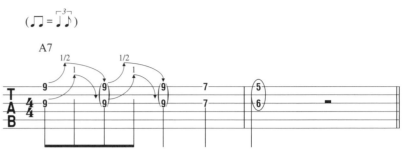

This next one features notes on strings 2 and 3 pre-bent by a half step and a whole step, respectively. Against the D note on top, the result is a Dm7 chord that's released to a G chord.

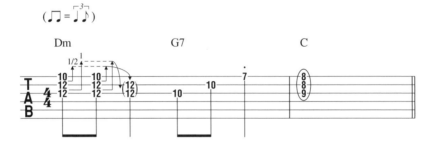

Slides

Since pedal steel guitar is played by *sliding* a steel bar across the strings, it only makes sense you can use legato slides to simulate pedal steel sounds. Combined with bends of multiple types and hybrid picking, things can get very pedal steel-sounding indeed. Here's one that climbs up a C chord via half-step slides and finishes off with some multiple bends.

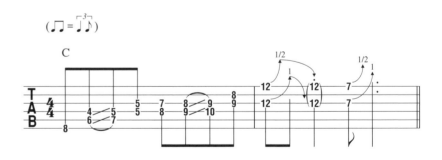

This next lick kicks off with a trio of double-stop slides to climb an A minor triad and finishes in grand fashion with a triple-stop bend. This one is quite twisted, but hey, that's what makes it fun!

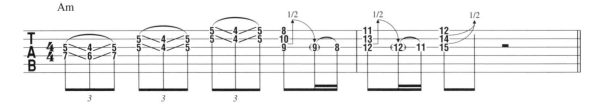

Chordal Bends

That last triple-stop bend leads us to our last topic: *chordal bends*. It's a bit of a misnomer, as we're actually going to bend notes on the outside edges of note groupings to form common chords. Here are some popular chord-type bends in the key of C.

First, here's a major form.

And here's the minor chord form.

And here's a major seven form, which would sound nice in a country ballad.

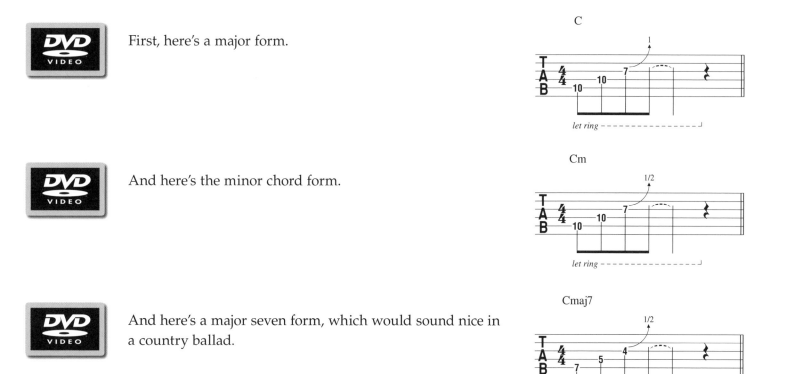

Let's put these to use in an A minor lick that makes a great closer. This lick has one other bend at the end that we didn't look at, but if you can nail the others so far, this one shouldn't give you any trouble.

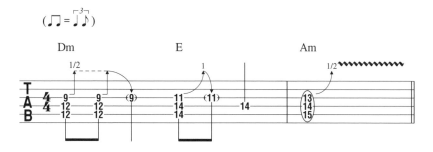

Here's a pedal-steel phrase you can use in a slow country waltz. Set in the key of C, this phrase outlines an F–C–G–C chord progression. You'll learn another chordal bend in this one as well—the G6 in measure 3 (beat 2).

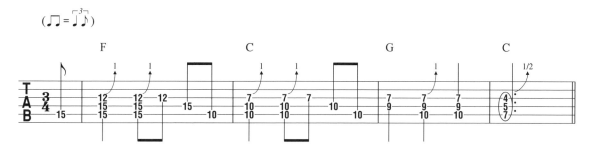

Other Bends

Don't forget to experiment. Just about anything you can play normally can be turned into a pedal steel-sounding bending lick if you just work at it long enough. We'll close out this section with a few more bending ideas that lend a pedal steel tinge to things. Some of these are just slight variations of ones we've covered already, but, as you'll see, the results can be vastly different.

This first bend is great for playing over dominant chords, because you're bending the ♭7th up to the root on string 2 against the 3rd on string 1. It looks like this in the key of A:

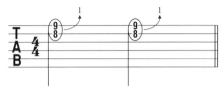

And here's how it sounds in a V–IV–I lick in D.

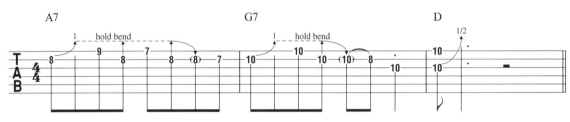

Here's another batch of sweet-sounding chordal bends that can turn a few heads. This one's in the key of D as well.

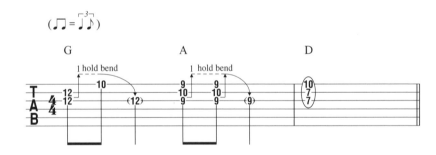

And let's go out in style with a multiple/oblique bend that'll really test your pedal steel emulation chops. This is similar to an earlier bend, but we've added a twist. Beginning with an A triad in root position, we simultaneously bend the 3rd (C♯) up a half step and bend the 5th (E) up a whole step while holding the root (A) steady. We repeat this move two frets lower for the G chord and then resolve to a first-inversion D chord that's delayed with a half-step bend and resolution. This one will take a bit of practice!

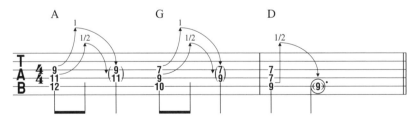

Well, there you go. You've now got the essential tools needed to make that axe of yours really sing. For more inspiration, check out the recordings of the pedal steel greats, like Buddy Emmons, Speedy West, and of more recent acclaim, Robert Randolph. Also check out Jerry Donahue, Danny Gatton, and other country guitar masters to hear these pedal steel licks in action. Cheers!